Lubbock Electric

Anne Elezabeth Pluto

Nixes Mate Books
Allston, Massachusetts

Book design by d'Entremont
Cover photograph by Anne Elezabeth Pluto

Special thanks to Philip Borenstein and Michael McInnis

ISBN 978-0-9993971-7-6

Nixes Mate Books
POBox 1179
Allston, MA 02134
nixesmate.pub/books

For Terry

Let's talk of graves, of worms and epitaphs,
Make durst our paper, and with rainy eyes
Write sorrow on the bosom of the earth.

William Shakespeare
Richard II

Contents

Lubbock Electric

Peregrine

Promethean
in sight in sound in thought in
deed – where you go, I follow
a paper trail now two decades long
I saved all your letters, the poems
written for the counties of the land
of 10,000 lakes, where I have never yet
been, what resplendent sorrow did we
arrive at what destination unticketed
unheard of did I not read you correctly
but only read what you could show, what
a play that was all comedy ending with
two weddings and now separation the ring
that binds loosens, I am drained of myself
held steadfast to the earth, tethered like some
great bird of prey, lessoned, kept on a lead
line, and now in flight, I fall, I falter, I keel
the appetite and nothing comes my way.

Banishment

(after Garcia Lorca)

I've thrown sand in the eyes of my horse
and still he finds his way back
to your door.

I've witnessed the crucifixion
of your interrupted heart
rend itself backwards
until your semen reached
me and I tasted myself
from your mouth.

I've tried to ride
far away
but *far* is only the future
and *away* simply a banishment
my horse still gallops
back to your door.

I've settled for silence
of the swiftest kind
all the lines to my heart
severed

the lines on my hands
dropped the reins of my horse
and watched
you walk
heavy and angry and hateful
into your next war.

Dementia Sonnet

Your mother thinks her sons are dead
but your older brother is getting ready
to rob the Bank of Texas – and you
have to save him before it happens – so
pull on your dead clothes, your Tony
Lama boots, grab that Winchester
and get him back – ride hard and fast:
pickup truck, pony express, 50 Mule
Team Borax long – you'd better make
up for lost time – good riddance
to bad feelings – just HURRY up – before he dies
shot through the heart by that sheriff – and
the dollar bills billow up across the
sand hot cap rock streets of Lubbock.

Flight of Ghosts

The incandescent evening
silver snow and hidden moon
opal light on houses imprisoned
by ice dams those stalagmite predators of
winter – you have made us a bold
people – up at dawn to shovel
cars and salt the paths
blow the snow into the air
spun like sugar falling softly
to cover what has already
been made ugly, grey, marked
with mud and tires – prodded
by plows – stomped down
with boots – the piles grow
steadily into battlements –
and rooks the birds
cry piteously overhead
circling wider and then
lost in the incandescent
evening – the final flight of
ghosts.

Love Letter to Lubbock

My desire
moves me west
mind of my making
I dreamt you
for decades
the sturdy blonde boy
on his father's panhandle
ranch – come what may
you lived another life
one I could not have
imagined – the road –
the music – the sensation
of consistent celebration
married young with
daughters – I wouldn't
have known how to even
speak – much less sing
you into my heart
my heart of the matter
you write me love
letters from Lubbock
God and the Devil
Jesus should come

to rapture – to you
to me – knit our very bones
together – a lifetime worth
of smiles – of mercy
to forgiveness
of knowing the meaning
of life – the final
fragility of fleeting fame
what you had – what I
dreamt – but now we meet
rancher's son
to blacksmith's daughter.
we meet without
the foolishness
of youth – without
the trappings of famous
others surrounding
just us – a man
and a woman
called back by life
called forth by love.

Texas Love Poem #2

Big is your heart
and grave to your making
I will set myself to your love
a thunder to the landscape
rain and flood and wild horses
in your father's corral
I am standing opposite your desire
slender and humid to be opened
kissed and made more than content
you are the very heart of Texas
never subdued but all ways
singing your self – soul to the tempo
soul of the story
soul of the earth
soul to my soul
heart of weeds and roses
play and sing
and dance me to the end.

Desire
(Texas Love Poem #3)

There's a flood in southeast
Texas and you tell me
it's been raining for two
days in Lubbock – three people
dead – the earth
drenched – I'll look beyond
and count the days
before you
arrive – it's now one
spin short of a full month
I'll count the miles as you fly first
to Houston and then east to me
I'll count each star that burns
the darkness into milk
each bird that moves
across the turning golden
trees outside my window
I've counted years from
my making – my child's birthday
in a row of candles
I've counted only on myself
to make life happen

to watch each cycle turn
with blood and light
but now I'll count with you
to make that moon shine splendid
against a boundless night.

A Phoenix Nest of Valentines
(Texas Love Poem #4)

The October light
sunrise early in the east
the black smoke sky on Venus
fire – orange and gold
the shiny crows gather
to the slender trees
a hawk circles
high and awake
I watch from inside
the cold morning calling me
out of my dreams.
I miss you already
before arrival
the sun hasn't risen yet
on you – the stars still give
Texas their light – when you hold
me in your hands imprint
their map onto my flesh
take up my open heart
in a phoenix nest
of new valentines
press me close

let your blood come hard
satisfy me into the future
brand me, the thunder of your heart
ignite me
and I will burn and burn
and burn
the luminous morning
out of night.

Lubbock Electric

Indiscriminate and irretrievable
the past splinters before us
like broken glass
there are times
when I am afraid to
move as if I will break
and break again your hands bind mine
against all that we have lost
alone – together – and found
by chance
by luck
in the name of god
at a time when all roads
led to the middle west – we see
each other without searching
I treasure even the minute
the clocks that do not work
unwound – left fallow to gather
up the splendid dust of hours spent
alone – together – the sound
of your heart against mine
the lights of Lubbock electric
all alight with midnight

fire – the dust rising from
the cotton cattle prairie
stretching out seemingly endless
Texas
I crave the future
haphazard mysterious
twisting out before me.

Gold

In the golden glow
your hair illuminates
the sleep tangled sheets
my hands pull through
gently wanting you
to wake up as I am
all ready for you
desirous to be
received again into your
final self. Now, I long for you
the winter hours
stretch across the blue black
sky – each tender memory remains lit
by each kiss you gave
by the sound of your voice
by the smell of your skin
by the salt milk
taste of consummation
my blood mixed between us
and the radiance of your eyes
that filled the small tight room
with independent light.

Outside Guthrie, Oklahoma

Hidden in high grass
only the iron–black horses, the
gate ornaments announce the
abandoned ranch – cool in
the early evening – prelude
to a storm – the horse pen
the white barns – now weathered
to ghost rides – the house
repainted – no longer anything
you once owned – the living
animals in the neighbor's pasture
mouse brown mare by the white
fence – her black mane
blows in the storm warning
wind – she rolls in delight
her back molds to the earth
her voice announces that she
sees us – we drive back
to the front gate – we cannot
enter what you sold
and left behind.

Playing Cards

The grey sky
punctuated with my yearning
by now, you would think that I
had learned enough about love
to know the glass is either
half full or half empty.
I call your name in my heart
and the reply is far flown
against the tumbleweed
where you are
and I am not yet arrived
I've put my heart to the test
supreme and lovely
and you have held it tight
before holding me
the silence is a field
of winter wheat that whispers
again and again and again
hold on to the future
believe in everything
this is what you have told me
what you have promised
send me your fear

I'll hold that too
against the grey sky
against my red scarf
and black cotton sweater
against my past
that come in spades
and diamonds – broken hearts
and blooming clubs
to haunt me.

Framed Twice

On my desk
the winter sun streams
through the third–floor windows.
You are there framed – twice.
Once
before we met
in another country
the sun in your eyes.
The second
after we had
found each other's heart
open and willing
you ride a bay horse
the prairie winds to the endless
horizon – your hair blown off you face
that looks away from the camera.

I've thrown the papers on the floor
in careless surrender – and step
around them – the clock hums on the wall
the music plays through me
the quiet room
my heart beating – 2000 miles west

between the photographs
the snow and ice comes as if to baptize
the winter hours
short days to long nights.
You will come
East
to me, the journey
of a star already risen
the sun behind you —the horse tethered
the milky way ahead
the silver moon in my hair
throw a rope around the constellations
and bring it all to me.

Lords of the Wichita
For Teresa

High grass to winter wheat
eastern horizon ending in pinpoint
precision on the Great Plains
after Christmas
the Buffalo come to feed
in the morning stumbling
forward nostrils flared in
the weak winter sunlight.
We search for them in the Wichita
mountain preserve wild longhorn
cattle graze in dry pastures – subtle
noses find what tastes best – spotted
hides and painted markings – calves
stray close to their mommas – and
all is still – hawks on treetops
perched – a lonely life of watching
time – deer bed down to catch
the high noon overhead – prairie
dogs protected too in the Wichita
peeking out at passersby – in the trees
hidden a longhorn bull chews patiently
grown into his great beauty waiting as the cow

eats; he has all the time in this world
for her and they will make another
spotted calf next spring the Buffalo
leave a trail – wet patties to trace
the course of their long protected
walk – we find them – a phalanx of five
heads tilted west as the wind stirs
the great prairie – giant as boulders
easily mistaken for Gods.

Someone Else's Dog-eared Script

Coming out of winter
slowly, the daylight lengthens
as the snow remains in sad
patches of items lost after Christmas
and patterns of dogs who ran outside
and came back in suddenly we are all
shoveling shit against the tidings of
this spring where I have lost track
of the daylight – falling asleep over
tests – on planes – driving 2 and a half
hours to travel 7 miles when I could be
halfway home – in a different life time was
more important – the winter made us vigilant
no longer surprised by envy – weary of sadness
carrying someone else's dog–eared script
in our pockets – it was enough to listen and
nod, politely at first, then shake in the huge
dismay of misunderstood connection – it was
more than enough to hide behind the behemoth
walls of snow and ice – to walk slowly on the shiny
black pavement – we took our lives in our hands
presenting them as gifts – a multitude of magi
lost astronomer kings of the east – each star

beckoned us forward – each coloring book constellation
was the map we threw down before the snows came
before the trains stopped running dead on long awaited
arrivals and we gave up –
retreating to our dimly lit homes and crackly telephones
anyone who dared to call us
sounded as though they were a trillion light years away.

Milk Moon

For Marc Statman

The moon is made of milk
a perfect round sphere,
a ball of spun silk stars trailing over
your favorite Brooklyn saloon the tar
roof beaches where skylights mark
the night like diamonds made of pointed
steel and isinglass – the anchored
ladder – the hanging mop – the chores
that spin us round like tops – the farewell
letters – the last look back – the sun
is rising on your folded maps – the
closing door – the brownstone stoop
the coming winter where you will
be no longer in the loop – the dark street
beckons towards the waiting train – the
light is fading – the waning moon
is made of milk
The perfect round sphere – a ball
of spun silk.

In Memory of Vail

Goodnight moon
Goodnight room
Goodnight to all
The horses yet to groom
Goodnight socks
Goodnight clocks
Goodnight to all
My cowgirl frocks
Goodnight dolls
And goodnight books
Goodnight to my riding hats
Hanging on hooks
Goodnight sister
Goodnight mother
Goodnight to my second father.
Goodnight house
And goodnight time
And all the sweet memory left behind
When next I wake, I'll still be nine.

Death Trap for Mermaids

I find the fish
hooks in the rug
stuck through and
shiny sharp a death
trap for mermaids I
work my fingers and
then resort to scissors
to cut them free.

I find the fish hook
line and sinker in
the rug muck of
the stream shiny death
for the sharp mermaid
scissors – she uses them
to set them free.

I find the mermaid fish hook
fancy tail stuck through
the line – the shiny stream of
a free death at sea.

Shakmati

I don't want to remember, but I
feel the incidents move through
me like water – muddy, murky, silt
on the bottom – bodies locked
in death embraces – we were stupid
I take that back where it belongs, the
heart cannot be commanded, at times
artfully restrained, but not told how
and what and where to move, there
are moments, when the present pain,
the despair of trial and error evades
me – what I have shaped, with my hands
and time, what I have reinvested in
removes itself by circumstance, then I
go backwards and wish I had not
moved at all.

Shakmati is Chess in Russian

Easter Sunday 2017

There are dead animals in the house
having crawled into a space that will
serve as both cradle and coffin – the sweet
sickly smell of decay coming through plaster
concrete, wood, insulation – no resurrection
this Easter I stop to imagine your terror:
shallow breathing – no space to turn and
retrace the journey in – the journey on
the smell will remain for at least a month
by then you will have become bone
part of the house – piece of the foundation
little ghost paws will make their way through
the walls and see what they can no longer
eat.

King's Chapel Burying Ground

The dead are pressed together
In the charnel house, an abundance
of ossuary riches, forgotten for centuries
turned to ditches, the crypts are sealed
off, each portal no longer has a door
but grass recedes to form a floor
in the cold spring evening, the electric hum
of skyscrapers distinguish us from the dead.

Green May

Copps Hill Burying Ground
10,000 thick bone stacked upon bone
to build the city – British
lobstermen in ghost light
used the hill as a battery – cannon
fodder to the Charlestown shore where
I had never walked there before
my periphery stopped at the skating
rink the oval circle on Commercial Street
a dollar entrance fee to find
the rhythm of eternal life skating eights in
imperfect time – this motion of forever
a path – a curve – a smooth surface cut
a pattern high above me on Copps Hill
the sun sets over the battery – the light
coming out from the lovely haunted homes – each
built with stolen slatestone foundations
the silence in locked spaces – green
May places –never look back – or fall
forward – the city is magnificently alive below.

What Ends Up Meaning Nothing

What ends up meaning
nothing – a missed train
a lost friend – traffic over
the bridge – through the
woods – a misplaced key
running out of milk – waking
up late – missing the friend
on the late train traffic moving
through milk – a bridge of nothing
across the traffic of the milky
way it ends.

Putney Bridge Station

You are the ghost that keeps on coming
up the stairs from the tube –
walking ahead of me on Putney Bridge
your hair reaches the edge of your collar
and I know that you have nowhere to go
destination unknown – the grass in the brick
overgrown – each footprint as quick as air
evaporating in front of me – a torrid column
smoke stack – burnt paper – another way
to always say *goodbye*.

Infinite Forever
For Colleen

The honey locust trees fan golden
out to cast the early October memory
of forgetting when I turned the heat
back on last year – this is a wide season
of painful repetition – time does not
matter – it's only the light caught between
what is tangible and what cannot remain
your death is another hole in the pattern
another birthday that will pass and pass
unnoticed – just a twinge of no regrets
and finality – hereditary heartbreak
and ghosts – would you call out through
the long and lonely corridor – hear the sound
of your boots in the snow – the city lit
up at midnight – we'll catch a glimpse
of our former selves in the plate glass
downtown Christmas window – it's the
photo no one ever took of us together –
stretches out into the infinite forever
how do I say words in love language
that only the dead can hear?

Mother Tender (2)

For Gloria Mindock

The bread in the forest
Is all eaten by birds – the path
Back home will flow without
Words – the darkest silence
Will be the picture of her – how you
Choose without choosing to remember
Her best – the laugh you will never stop
To forget – the hopeful place where there
can never be regret – the smell of her books
The chances you took – the final look
Backwards – mother tender – what you will
Never fail to remember – remains.

The Home Borough

Grandmother then in your 1st
century of relative oblivion
Brooklyn was still a Dutch
word and farms littered
the view, I never saw
this, save in vast exception
ghost light memory haunts
the quiet photographs – silver
alum paper – and names
of graves long grown
over this pattern
a warp threaded to
a symmetric imperfection
Easter linens hidden
in deep lavender, the nocturnal
map of the stars that plow
the milky light over
the East River cross town
traffic to the Hudson the D
Train ran then – express to
The Bronx – an orange circle
a million bodies crushed
into metal containers

we were the cattle
of Brooklyn, learning
to hide behind newspapers
on the IRT – change at Atlantic
count the stops
read the graffiti – the gang
tags and piss tight smell
of Church Ave station
on the lonely end of St. Paul's
Place and Caton Ave
where Caledonian Hospital was
nestled between apartment
buildings thick near the park
we drank White Rock Ginger ale
on Sundays with mom and dad
strange streets as the map spread
into green mystery a lake of landing
birds I counted the horses lazily
trotting the perimeter each tail
pushing away a jungle
of flies the streets, the park
and the lake remain – the hospital closed
in sad distain the quantity of living

calling me forward all the souls
converge in luscious shadow
repair and hope
masquerade and first love, that pain
the lingering absolute, that too
became a shade, a fable, the exquisite
insight you brought to the table
when I was longing to escape and be
the heroine
in my own story.

Salt Memory

Winter salt
consummate ice
February melt
memory dull
sublunary love
my childhood
home the snow
settles into our
bones, our homes
our hearts divided
by decades, as I reach
out your silence pushes
back an eternity
of haste – you cannot
escape the cold
snow in Georgia
ice in the Carolinas – sunny
Florida heat rising
where you could
retire early – 9/11
the ash shifting smell
of the dead
the far away

tremble for a
lost adventure
I came home
you know I came
home to check
on my parents
I came home to
see the city smolder
across the river
in Brooklyn found
your fire
station at dusk
reading the names
of the lost – you were
not among them.
First Love
the boy who cheated
suicide twice the sailor
the fireman
you never knew how
I came
to know
that you were still alive.

Autumn

An hour in the yard – man with a machine
blow the leaves into a carpet of red, brown,
orange, then gold – change blades and
mulch – the bag fills with dust – clouds
of summer dirt kicked up in your wake
the leaves transformed to fall confetti spread as loam
a blanket for the snow to take and hold
the steel gray sky slips behind the houses
on the low road – I know your pain
is unbearable and yet you bear it in the
dust with the dog behind you – I'd rake
them all without your help – my rhythm
established long ago – lonely autumn tasks
stacking wood – raking leaves – arranging
the shed – covering the glass topped
table from the impending storm – predicable
and bold as the unsteady future.

Contortionist

Driving
in low light
the nocturnal day
of small creatures
I see him
creep across
the road
ambling raccoon
downshift
into 2nd
parallel to the
double yellow
line he rolls
a perfect ball
of autumn fur
I can't shift
into 1st – taken
into the light
of high beams
from the road
behind – he is rolling
now – a contortionist
pained the next day –

I return
no blood
no road kill carcass
sigh of
relief until
I change
direction – there
buried
in the leaves
chameleon
raccoon
perfect
ball of cold fur.

Towards the Solstice

The sun fades
early in the east
we turn on lights
and cook our dinner
in muted colors birds
sing less frequently
now as the darkness
rapidly arrives dusk
at 6:30 night and moon
and dream by 8:00 the
cicadas beating their wings
in unison from the highest trees.

Twelfth Night

In the dark the crescent
moon illuminates the road
the river and my retreat.
I'm heavy with stagnation
no room to move
in either direction.
Let Mary take my place
and I will be her icon
assume the silent
knowledge the moment
of birth and joy
the precious baby whose fate
She didn't think of when
turbaned kings laid gold at her feet.
Silent Mary holy Mary
You can have my heart
in exchange for your peace
it's indignant and damaged
but you've seen worse
take it from me
fill its fissures with gold
seal them with myrrh
and frankincense will signify

the holiday.
Wear it as a jewel
and take my place.
I will hold your son
against my empty chest
His heart strong enough
to keep us both alive.

Christmas

I'd gladly follow them
Three men from the east
having watched the moon and stars
forever searching from their Persian tower
where now their tombs stand turquoise
studded blue reaching heaven – did it burn them
into splendor when they packed their gifts
and saddled camels for the journey west
and could He really have still been newborn
or was He already his mother's splendid son
whose uncommon life and violent death had yet to
open – a book we all have read and read again.
This Christmas the story passes through me as if you
had entered – welcome home this star it burns for me
as you – brilliant golden –
the light you bring me from the west
your skin as it ignites my own and turned together
into the rope of our surrender – I'd gladly follow you
this Christmas to any manger – where they came too
and brought their gifts –
for a healer, a holy man, a king.

Acknowledgments

Special Thanks to Jeffery Side and Argotist Ebooks for publishing the first incarnation of *Lubbock Electric* in 2013.
The following poems first appeared there: "Love Letter to Lubbock", "Texas Love Poem #2", "Desire (Texas Love Poem #3)", "A Phoenix Nest of Valentines (Texas Love Poem #4)", "Lubbock Electric", "Gold", "Christmas", "Outside Guthrie", "Oklahoma", "Playing Cards", "Framed Twice", "Banishment", and "Twelfth Night"

"Peregrine" first appeared in *Shadows of the Future: An Otherstream Anthology* – Argotist Ebooks.

"Towards the Solstice", "Dementia Sonnet", "Easter Sunday 2017", "King's Chapel Burying Ground", "Green May", and "Putney Bridge Station" first appeared in the *Mockingheart Review*.

"Lords of the Wichita" first appeared in the *Nixes Mate Review*.

"Shakmati" first appeared in *@poetry2go*.

About the Author

Anne Elezabeth Pluto is Professor of Literature and
Theatre at Lesley University in Cambridge, MA
where she is founder of *Commonthought Magazine*
and the artistic director and one of the founders
of the Oxford Street Players. She is an alumna of
Shakespeare & Company, and has been a member of
the Worcester Shakespeare Company since 2011. She
was a member of the Boston small press scene in the
late 1980s and is one of the founders and editors at
Nixes Mate Review. Her chapbook, *The Frog Princess*,
was published by White Pine Press (1985), and her
chapbook *Benign Protection* by Cervena Barva Press
(2016). Recent publications include: *The Buffalo
Evening News, Unlikely Stories: Episode IV, Mat Hat Lit,
Pirene's Fountain, The Enchanting Verses Literary Review,
MockingHeart Review, Yellow Chair Review, Levure
Litteraire – numero 12, The Naugatuck River Review,
Tuesday, An Art Project, the Muddy River Review.*

Nixes Mate Books features small-batch artisanal literature, created by writers that use all 26 letters of the alphabet and then some, honing their craft the time-honored way: one line at a time.

Other or Forthcoming Nixes Mate titles:

nixesmate.pub/books

CPSIA information can be obtained
at www.ICGtesting.com
Printed in the USA
LVHW081749070120
642794LV00016B/1498/P

9 780999 397176